An Unofficial Activity Book
Awesome Activities for Fans of Animal Crossing

Word Searches, Code-Breakers, and Matching Games to Improve Your Skills

Jen Funk Weber

Sky Pony Press
New York

Copyright © 2020 by Hollan Publishing, Inc.

Animal Crossing® and Animal Crossing: New Horizons® are trademarks of Nintendo.

The Animal Crossing and Animal Crossing: New Horizons games are copyright © Nintendo.

Sky Pony Press books may be purchased in bulk at special discounts for sales promotion, corporate gifts, fund-raising, or educational purposes. Special editions can also be created to specifications. For details, contact the Special Sales Department, Sky Pony Press, 307 West 36th Street, 11th Floor, New York, NY 10018 or info@skyhorsepublishing.com.

Sky Pony® is a registered trademark of Skyhorse Publishing, Inc.®, a Delaware corporation.

Visit our website at www.skyhorsepublishing.com.

10 9 8 7 6 5 4 3 2 1

Cover art licensed by Shutterstock.com
Puzzles created by Jen Funk Weber
Interior art by Grace Sandford,
   additional art licensed by Shutterstock.com.
Book design by Noora Cox

Print ISBN: 978-1-5107-6306-7

Printed in the United States of America

Table of Contents

Find Your Dream Bed

Practice customizing furniture. Start at the red arrow. If you collect all three customization kits before you make it to the finish, you can choose a new bed design. Which of the four is your favorite? Circle it and imagine adding it to your island home.

Fast Track Gaming

Start at the red arrow. Write every third letter on the spaces until all have been used. If you place them correctly, you'll reveal a tip for speeding up some Animal Crossing steps.

P _ _ _ _ _   _   _ _   _ _   _ _ _ _   _ _ _ _

_ _ _ _ _ _ _

Crafty Neighbors

What can you learn from your crafty neighbors? To find out, circle the names of 11 raw materials in the word search. They might be forward, backward, up, down, or diagonal. Write unused letters on the blank spaces to discover a handy tip.

Hint: Circle each letter of the words you find so you can find the leftover letters more easily.

T	T	O	O	B	T	C	R	A	F	
R	T	S	D	E	E	W	I	N	I	
E	U	G	V	N	G	I	D	R	L	
E	L	S	O	A	G	G	O	E	O	
B	R	T	T	S	U	N	O	M	O	
R	S	A	Y	E	N	S	W	H	B	
A	C	A	R	U	D	E	D	T	M	
N	H	L	G	E	L	P	R	I	A	
C	R	G	A	R	O	E	A	C	B	
H	E	I	P	Y	G	E	H	R	S	
T	D	O	O	W	T	F	O	S	T	

- BAMBOO
- BOOT
- CLAY
- GOLD NUGGET
- HARDWOOD
- IRON NUGGET
- RUSTED PART
- SOFTWOOD
- STONE
- TREE BRANCH
- WEEDS

____ _____ _____ ____

_____ _____ ___

6

The Gift of Gab

If you like chatting with friends while you play Animal Crossing New Horizons, this app is for you. Cross off every instance of a letter that appears three times—and only three times. The first one's been done for you. Write the remaining letters on the spaces, in order from left to right and top to bottom, to receive the gift of gab.

E	N	A	O	D̸
O	K	D̸	L	P
D̸	P	I	E	N
A	E	A	K	P

Use this to text and chat with friends in-game:

___ ___ ___ ___   ___ ___ ___ ___

Who's Who

Match the Animal Crossing character to its job and get to know them a little better. The next time you have a problem, you'll know exactly who to visit!

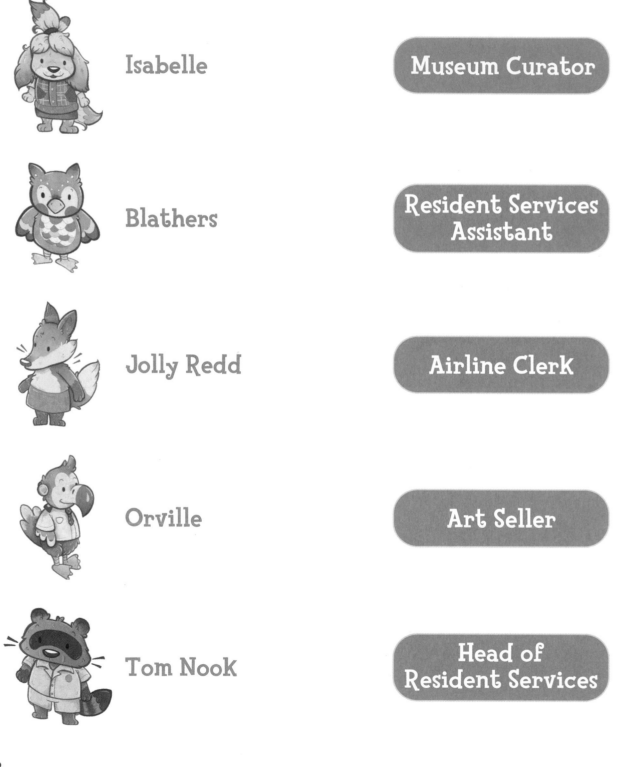

Isabelle

Blathers

Jolly Redd

Orville

Tom Nook

Museum Curator

Resident Services Assistant

Airline Clerk

Art Seller

Head of Resident Services

Recipe for Recycling

Here's an excellent way to use trash you fish out of the ocean and rivers. Only one of the recipes on the left is correct and leads to an item shown on the right. Can you figure out which is the correct recipe?

1 empty can
1 boot
1 iron nugget

1 empty can
1 boot
1 old tire

1 empty can
2 boots
1 book

Recycled
Can Thumb
Piano

Succulent
Plant

Trash Bags

Fossil Finder

Boxes connected by lines contain the same letter. Some letters are given, but others have to be guessed. Fill in all the boxes to reveal today's fossil finds.

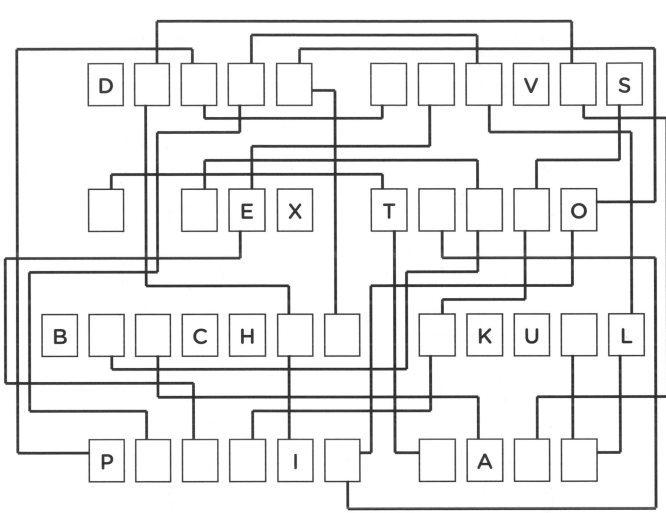

GAMING TIP: You can dig up four fossils per island per day. If you want more than four, visit another island.

Cranky Characters

Place the 6 character names in the crossword. Use the number of letters and intersecting letters to figure out where each word logically fits. Transfer the numbered letters to the spaces at the bottom of the page to finish the fun fact.

5 Letters	8 Letters
~~FLASH~~	HAMPHREY
O'HARE	OCTAVIAN
TWIRP	VLADIMIR

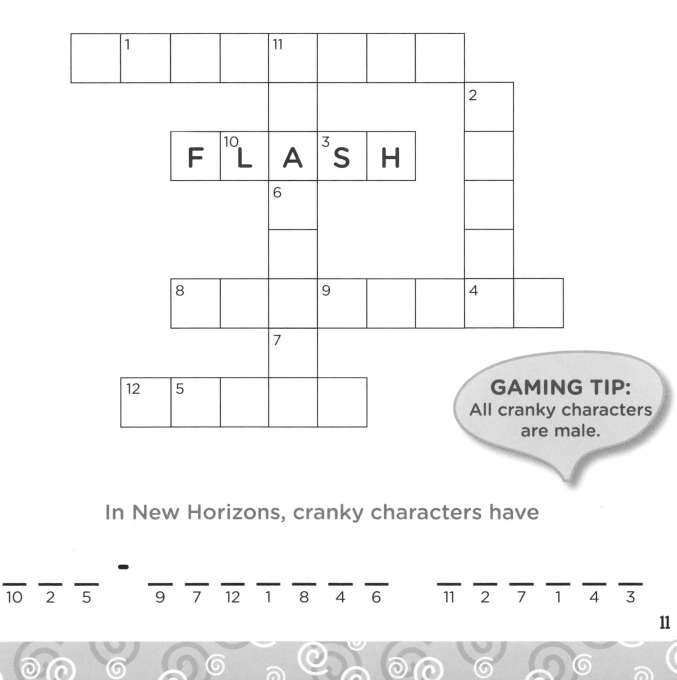

GAMING TIP:
All cranky characters are male.

In New Horizons, cranky characters have

‾‾ ‾‾ ‾‾ ▬ ‾‾ ‾‾ ‾‾ ‾‾ ‾‾ ‾‾ ‾‾   ‾‾ ‾‾ ‾‾ ‾‾ ‾‾ ‾‾
10 2   5   9 7 12 1 8 4 6   11 2 7 1 4 3

Piece of Wisdom

Friends can actually help you get some items you want in the game. Discover how by finding the five puzzle pieces that fit the shapes in the rectangle. Watch out! Pieces might be rotated or flipped. Write the letters of the correct pieces on the spaces. Not all pieces are used. If you place the pieces correctly, you'll learn an easier way to obtain hard-to-find items.

Do this to get items you want or need.

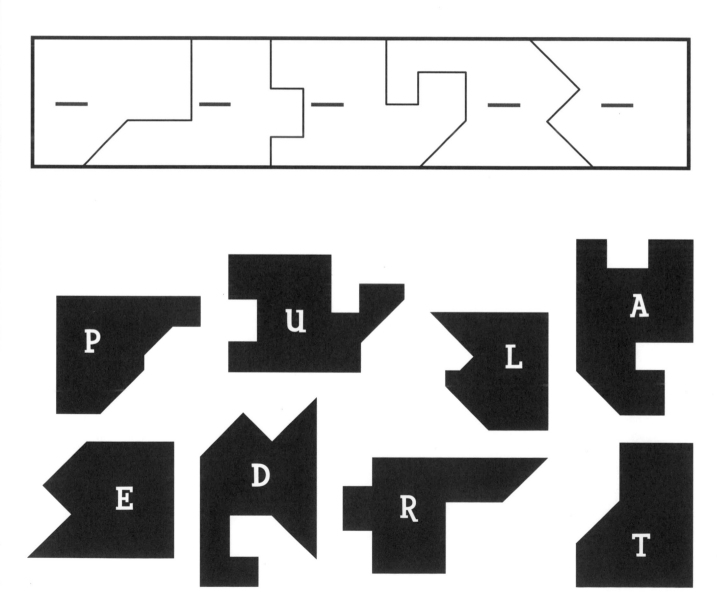

Art Appraisal 1

Redd the fox will try to sell you a fake painting instead of the original, but don't let him trick you. Find the differences between the original painting and Redd's forged painting below and circle them. Use this skill to help you get the most out of your art purchases.

Wand-ering

Start at the top left of this maze to determine which item is one of the ingredients you need to make a star wand.

GAMING TIP: During a meteor shower, look for Celeste the owl to get new wand recipes!

14

One to Grow On

Color by number to find out what grows when you plant a coconut on the beach in Animal Crossing New Horizons.

1 YELLOW   **3** GREEN   **5** DARK BLUE

2 BROWN   **4** LIGHT BLUE

Money Rock Mystery

To earn extra bells in Animal Crossing and unlock cool new features, it helps to know which items give you an advantage. One such item is the money rock, which you can look for every day. Read the clues below to figure out which of the rocks is the money rock.

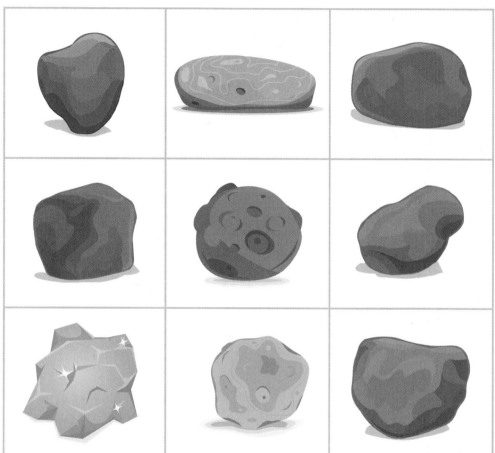

Clues:

1. The money rock is either in the bottom row, the left column, or a corner square.

2. The money rock is not in a column of gray rocks.

3. The money rock shares two borders with two non-gray rocks, but is not above one.

GAMING TIP:
If you find the money rock each day and strike it with your shovel, you can collect up to 16,000 bells!

Resource Radar

Why should sparkle spots, Earth stars, and tiny water spouts be on your radar? To find out, cross off every instance of a letter that appears three times—and only three times. The first one is done for you. Write the remaining letters on the spaces, in order from left to right and top to bottom, to reveal why these things are important.

H	N	B	G	U	Y	R	E
Z	A	W	H	T	P	L	K
U	A	Y	C	N	Z	E	S
W	B	T	K	O	D	U	W
I	K	Z	G	Y	N	B	H

Sparkle spots, Earth stars, and water spouts are

__ __ __ __ __   __ __ __ __ __ __

__ __   __ __ __

Catch This

Can you catch these seven bugs in the word search? They might be forward, backward, up, down, or diagonal. If you can locate and contain them, the remaining letters will reveal something these insects have in common to help you find and catch them in the game.

Hint: Circle the letters instead of the whole word so you can see the leftover letters more easily.

```
D R A G O N F L Y
G A C A H T C L H
N A M L O L F T H
I E S S N R E C Ⓜ
W Y L F E R I F Ⓞ
D R I T Y L T T Ⓣ
R E T R B S F W Ⓗ
I U H I E L E L T
B H E Y E F L Y Y
```

BIRDWING
BUTTERFLY
DAMSELFLY
DRAGONFLY
FIREFLY
HONEYBEE
~~MOTH~~

_ _ _ _ _ _   _ _ _   _ _ _ _ _

_ _ _ _ _ _ _ _   _ _ _ _ _   _ _ _ _ _

The Power of Three

Find your way to a 3-star rating. The quickest, best way from Start to Finish has you pass through three things you need to do to get a 3-star rating and a visit from K. K. Slider.

START

Make a custom pattern

Wish on a star

Build bridges

Get more villagers

Plant flowers

FINISH

GAMING TIP: Keep checking with Isabelle. She'll tell you what you need to do to increase your island rating.

Message in a . . . *Math Problem?*

Boxes connected by black lines contain the same letter. Some letters are given, but others have to be guessed. Fill in all the boxes to reveal which clues add up to a new message just for you.

Tooling Around

Place the six tools in the crossword. Use the number of letters and intersecting letters to figure out where each word logically fits. Transfer the numbered letters to the spaces at the bottom of the page. If you fill in the puzzle correctly, you'll get a gaming tip!

6 Letters	9 Letters	11 Letters
LADDER	GOLDEN AXE	COLORFUL NET
~~SHOVEL~~	SLINGSHOT	WATERING CAN

This tool will keep you organized and ready to act in a jiffy:

___ ___ ___ ___   ___ ___ ___ ___
7   3   3   4   6   1   2   5

Cha-ching

Discover how to get richer by finding the eight puzzle pieces that fit the shapes in the rectangle. Watch out! Pieces might be rotated or flipped. Write the letters of the correct pieces on the spaces. Not all pieces are used. Read the letters on the spaces to reveal a way to double your bell income.

Mood Master

Reaction symbols are a fun way to express your feelings to other players. Match the reaction symbol to the emotion it expresses.

Joy

Sadness

Anger

Greet-ings

Shocked

Delight

Dodo Destinations

Three Animal Crossing New Horizons players (Jillibean, Bell Farmer, and Sparkle Ferret) are venturing out on Mystery Island Tours. What kind of island does each player encounter? Find your way through the maze to find out.

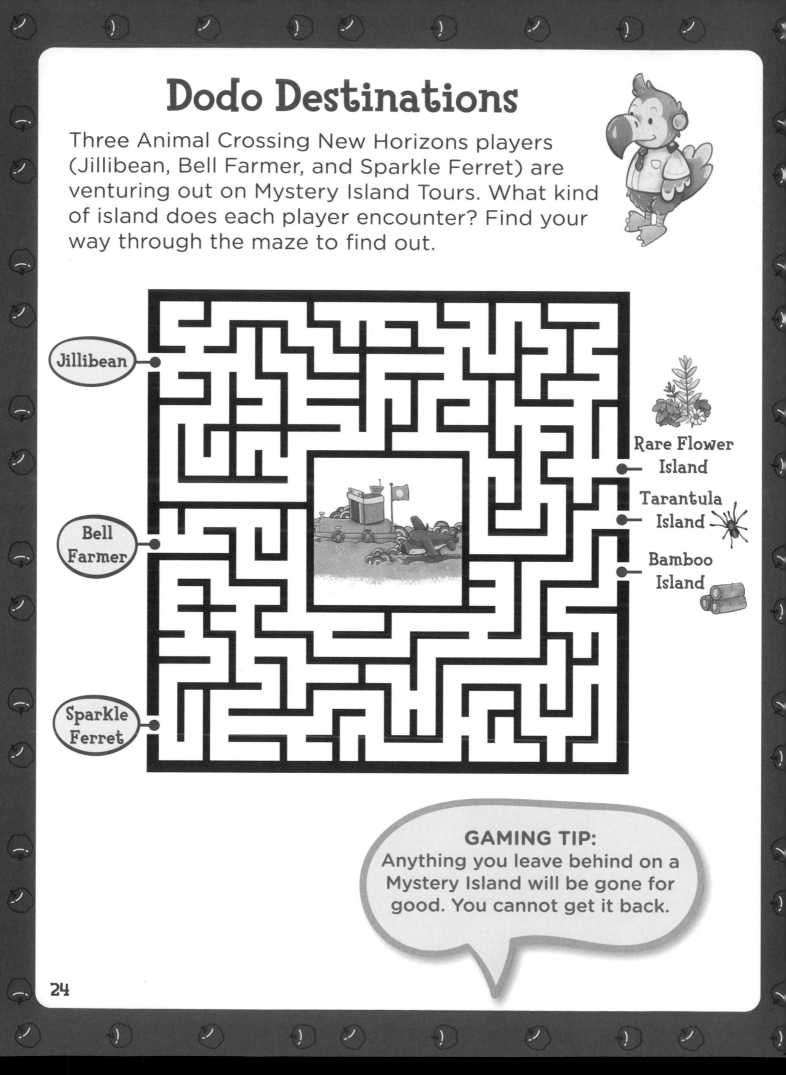

Jillibean

Bell Farmer

Sparkle Ferret

Rare Flower Island

Tarantula Island

Bamboo Island

GAMING TIP:
Anything you leave behind on a Mystery Island will be gone for good. You cannot get it back.

Make It Yours

Start at the ⬇. Write every third letter on the spaces until all have been used. If you place them correctly, you'll reveal one way to personalize your New Horizons island.

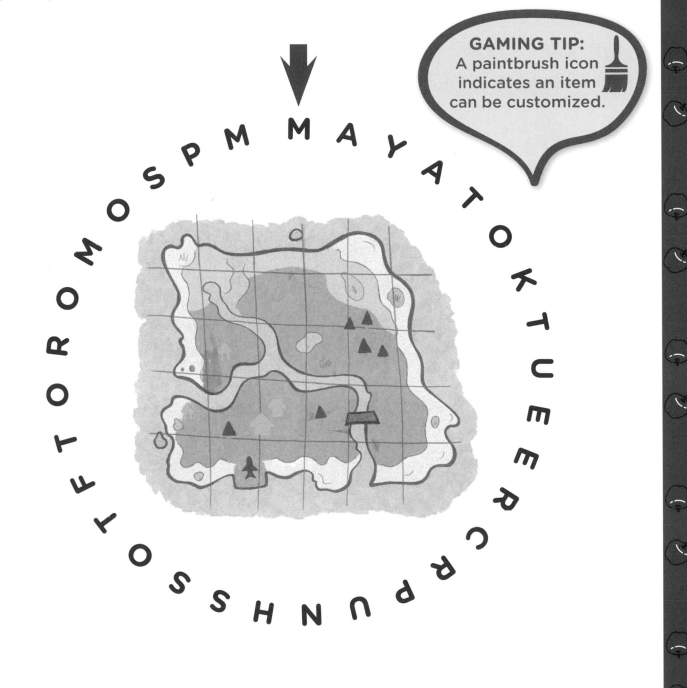

⬇

O S P M   M   M A Y A T O K T U E
T O R O M O   E
F T O R O M O S P M   R
                               C
                               R
                               P
S O L F T   P
  S S H N N U P P R C R E   U
                             N N

(Letters arranged in a circle, clockwise from the arrow: M A Y A T O K T U E E R C R P P U N N H S S O L F T O R O M O S P M)

> **GAMING TIP:** A paintbrush icon 🖌 indicates an item can be customized.

M _ _ _   _ _ _   _ _ _ _ _ _

_ _ _ _ _ _ _

Year-Round Residents

Can you find the nine year-round critters in the word search? They might be forward, backward, up, down, or diagonal. If you can locate them all you'll reveal a repeating mystery word!

Hint: Circle each letter instead of the whole word so it's easier to see the letters left over.

B L I A N S U G B H

U G R B U M G B E C

(F) U G E P B O R U A

(L) B G S D B M T U O

(Y) G A B U I G B H R

U W G G T B P U G F

B U G C W B U S G R

B U R G B O U G B A

U A G B U G R B U H

B G B A N T U M G W

ANT
BAGWORM
~~FLY~~
HERMIT CRAB
MOTH
SNAIL
SPIDER
WASP
WHARF ROACH

GAMING TIP:
Some critters in New Horizons are present only during a few months or a season. Others, like the Citrus Long-horned Beetle, are present year-round.

The mystery word is

_____ .

26

Get Rich Quick!

Getting rich in Animal Crossing New Horizons is a snap if you achieve this one goal. To find out what that goal is, cross off every instance of a letter that appears three times—and only three times. The first one's done for you. Write the remaining letters on the spaces, in order from left to right and top to bottom, to reveal a tip.

T	D	M	U	V	R	N
K	I	P	G	D	C	O
A	X	V	M	L	B	U
X	Y	C	L	O	K	W
S	E	D	X	L	L	H
M	V	I	G	K	H	C

If you can do this in New Horizons, you'll get rich quick!

_ _ _ _ _ _ _   _ _ _ _ :

_ _ _   _ _ _   _ _ _ _   _ _ _ _

Art Appraisal 2

Redd the fox will try to sell you a fake painting instead of the original, but don't let him trick you. Find the difference between the original painting and Redd's forged painting below and circle it. Use this skill to help you get the most out of your art purchases.

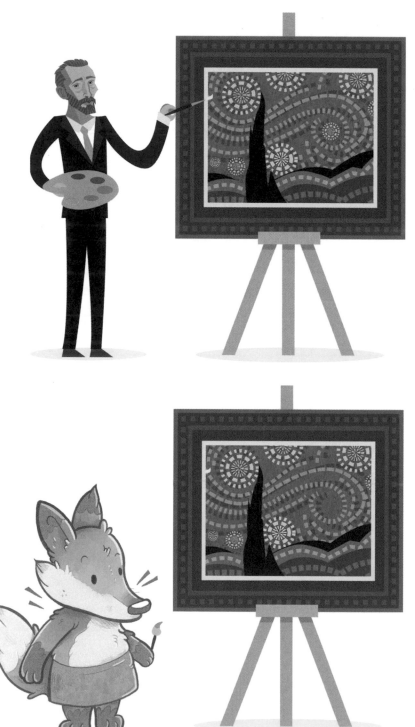

Green Thumb Enterprise

A money tree can help you grow 10,000 bells into 30,000 bells! Find your way through this maze by passing through the steps necessary to grow a money tree.

GAMING TIP: 10,000 bells is the maximum you can plant to reliably triple your investment.

START

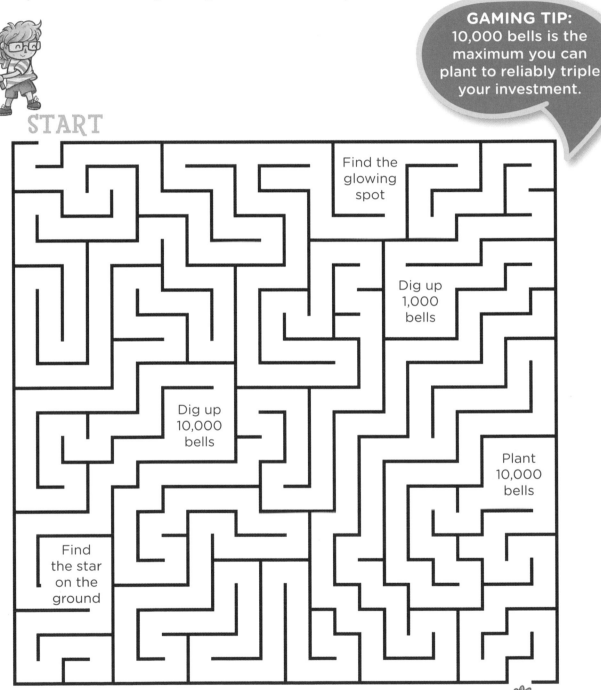

Find the glowing spot

Dig up 1,000 bells

Dig up 10,000 bells

Plant 10,000 bells

Find the star on the ground

Connect the Dots

Connect the dots to discover a fish you can catch in the game.

10

9   11

40

39   8   12

3   4   5   6   7   13

38   14

2

37   15

1   17

36   18

35   16   19

32   34   31   30   33   20   21

29   26   25   22

28   27   24   23

FUN FACT:
You can get
3,000 bells for
catching it!

The Greatest Rock Hits

Place the six rock-based resources and items in the crossword. Use the number of letters and intersecting letters to figure out where each word logically fits. The first one's been done for you. Transfer the numbered letters to the spaces at the bottom of the page. If you fill in the puzzle correctly, you'll discover a way to maximize the loot you get from rocks.

4 Letters	5 Letters
CLAY	SHELF
GOLD	STONE
~~IRON~~	
WELL	

GAMING TIP:
Rock resources are important ingredients in DIY recipes.

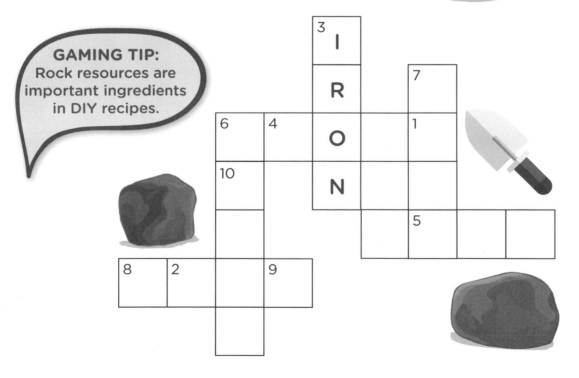

Do this to ensure you can hit a rock 8 times quickly:

__ __ __   __ __ __   __ __ __ __ __
9 3 8   4 7 2   10 2 5 1 6

31

You're Invited!

You're invited to visit a friend's island to bring back some cherry trees, which are not native to your island. First, however, you'll need this. Discover what "this" is by finding the eight puzzle pieces that fit the shapes in the rectangle. Watch out! Pieces might be rotated or flipped. Write the letters of the correct pieces on the spaces. Not all pieces are used.

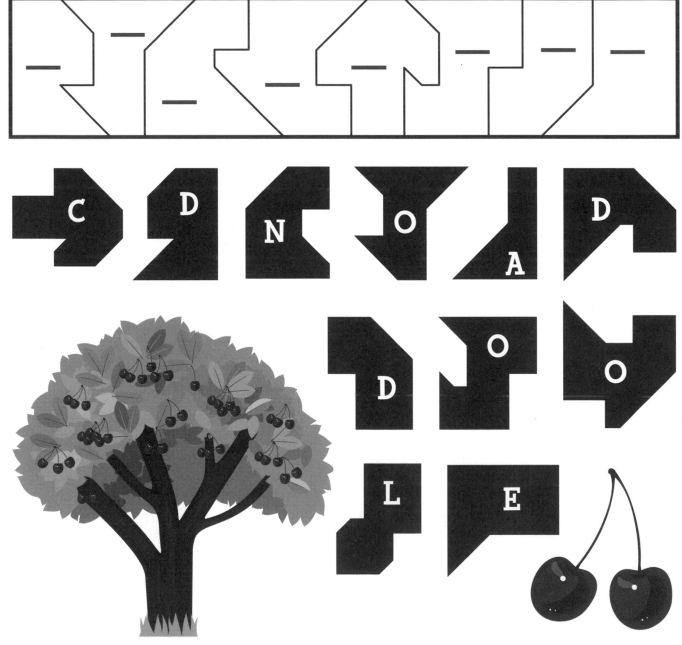

Fishing Skills Challenge

Catching a wide variety of fish is one of the many challenges in Animal Crossing, so it's key to be able to identify the shape of different fish underwater before casting your line. Have fun matching these fish to their shadowy shapes so you can take your fishing to the next level!

Starry Night

You wished on a star last night in Animal Crossing New Horizons. Can you find your way to the beach to collect star fragments?

GAMING TIP: The first time you meet Celeste the owl (after 7 p.m.), she'll give you a star wand.

START

FINISH

Temporary Treats

Start at the ↓. Write every third letter on the spaces until all have been used. If you place them correctly, you'll reveal advice you don't want to miss.

G___ ___ - __ - _ - ____ _____ __ _____ _____

Tent Dilemma

A puzzle-loving friend has agreed to move to your island, but only if you set up the tent of her choice. Can you read the clues to figure out which of these nine tents your friend wants?

Clues:

1. The tent I want is pointy at the top.

2. The tent I want does not have a flag.

3. The tent I want is an even-numbered tent.

GAMING TIP:
Don't fret about where you put your tent. You can move your house later if you want.

Maxed Museum

To get the rest of the gaming tip below, cross off every instance of a letter that appears three times—and only three times. The first one is done for you. Write the remaining letters on the spaces, in order from left to right and top to bottom, to reveal one requirement you'll have to meet to complete your museum collection.

I	K	F	W	P	C	H	L
A	Y	H	Q̸	G	Y	K	B
Q̸	B	E	F	I	C	A	R
R	G	W	H	O	U	Q̸	G
K	F	C	N	B	I	D	W

GAMING TIP:
You need to donate 60 fish, bugs, and fossils before Blathers will add an art wing to the museum.

If you want a complete museum collection,
you'll have to do this:

__ __ __ __ - __ __ __ __ __

Say What?

Look for these weird words in the word search. They might be forward, backward, up, down, or diagonal. If you can locate them all, the remaining letters will reveal what kind of words they are.

Hint: Circle the letters of each word instead of the whole word so it's easier to see the leftover letters.

S	P	U	R	R	T	Y	L
R	C	A	T	T	M	O	I
E	E	R	P	R	O	N	K
Z	O	H	C	M	O	H	E
Z	P	H	C	R	R	A	W
U	S	A	E	O	V	S	H
F	M	(G)	(N)	(I)	(O)	(B)	O
Z	I	P	Z	O	O	M	A

~~BOING~~
FUZZERS
LIKE WHOA
MACMOO
MOOCHER
PRONK
PURRTY
VROOM
ZIP ZOOM
ZORT

These 10 "words" are

_____ .

Tulip Time

What do you get when you cross two orange tulips in Animal Crossing? Follow the maze to discover the result.

GAMING TIP: Flowers need water to create a hybrid.

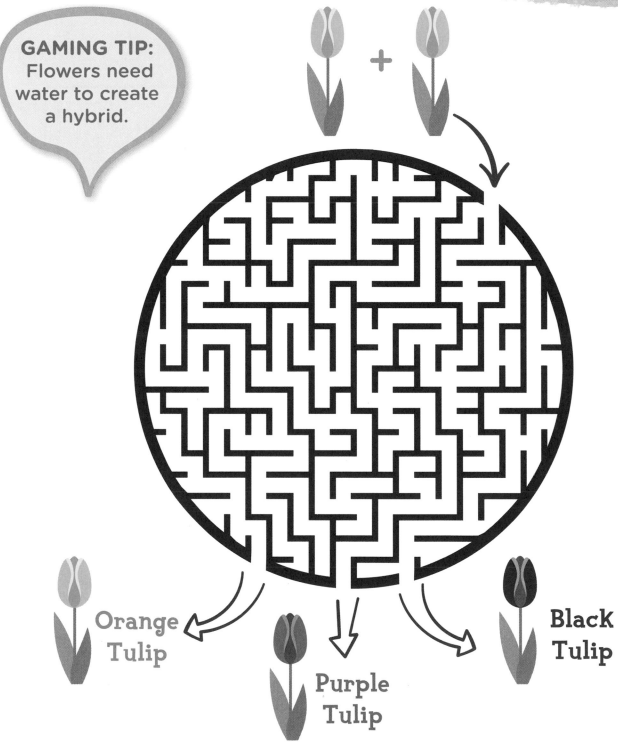

Orange Tulip

Purple Tulip

Black Tulip

What's Shakin'?

What's shakin'? You are! And with good reason. Find out why by filling in the squares. Boxes connected by lines contain the same letter. Some letters are given, but others have to be guessed. Fill in all the boxes and get a gaming tip.

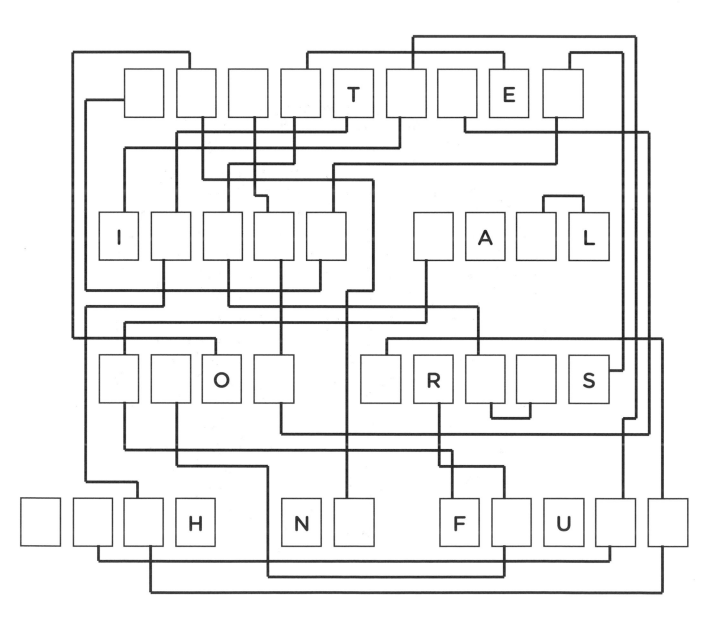

Not For Sale

Place the seven items in the crossword. Use the number of letters and intersecting letters to figure out where each word logically fits. Transfer the numbered letters to the spaces at the bottom of the page. If you fill in the puzzle correctly, you'll discover a way you might get something cool to add to your wardrobe.

7 Letters	8 Letters	14 Letters
BANDAGE	EYE PATCH	CANDY-SKULL MASK
CAT NOSE	NOSE DRIP	
MONOCLE	PACIFIER	

GAMING TIP: Some items in Animal Crossing New Horizons are not for sale; they're only available at certain times under certain circumstances.

If you give away your

14 4 6 9 2 12 5 13   3 10 7 3 5 11 1 8

you might get

14 4 6 9 2 12 5 13   8 2 5 12 1 8

41

Self Improvement

Find out what you need to change your look by finding the seven puzzle pieces that fit the shapes in the rectangle. Watch out! Pieces might be rotated or flipped. Write the letters of the correct pieces on the spaces to discover the name of the item.

Hint: Not all pieces are used. Read the letters on the spaces to reveal the simple thing you need to make self-improvement changes.

GAMING TIP:
You can create this mystery item with a DIY recipe, get it as a prezzie, or buy it.

Art Appraisal 3

Redd the fox will try to sell you a fake painting instead of the original, but don't let him trick you. Find the difference between the original painting and Redd's forged painting below and circle it. Use this skill to help you get the most out of your art purchases.

Connect the Dots

Connect the dots to see how you can get to another island in the game.

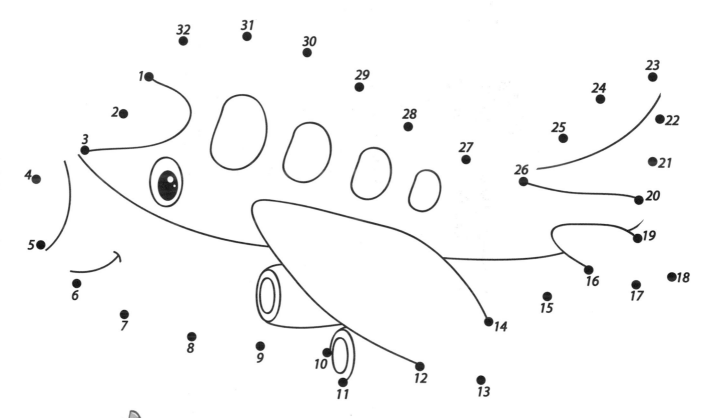

Heads Up: Incoming

Don't you hate missing out on a balloon present because you don't see it coming? Stay ready for surprise balloons with this handy trick and grab every floating prezzie headed your way. Start at the ↓. Write every third letter on the spaces until all have been used. If you place them correctly, you'll know when a balloon is near, even if you don't see it.

GAMING TIP:
Use your slingshot to break balloons so you can retrieve the present, but don't break the balloon over water.

L I S T E N   F O R   A

W H I S T L I N G   B R E E Z E

What's "Normal"?

In Animal Crossing New Horizons, characters with a "normal" personality share a common interest. To find out what this interest is, find the names of the 10 normal characters in the word search. They might be forward, backward, up, down, or diagonal. If you can locate them all, the remaining letters reveal this common interest.

Hint: Circle the letters of the words instead of the whole word so it's easier to see the leftover letters.

```
(V) (I) (C) (H) (E)  Y  T  N
 V   H   E   A  N  Y  O  A
 E   U   G   N  E  R  E  M
 S   L   U   N  M  E  L  S
 T   S   L   A  I  L  K  K
 A   N   A   V  L  Y  S  E
 T   O   R   A  E  A  E  A
 D   N   O   S  E  G  A  Y
```

GAYLE
MERENGUE
NORMA
NOSEGAY
SAVANNAH
SKYE
SUNNY
SYLVANA
VESTA
~~VICHE~~

___ ___ ___ ___ ___ ___ ___ ___ ___ ___ ___ ___ ___ ___ ___ ___ ___ ___ ___ ___

Know Before You Go

Whoa! Before you head out on that Mystery Island Tour, figure out the mystery message so you can make the most of your journey. Cross off every instance of a letter that appears three times—and only three times. The first one's done for you. Write the remaining letters on the spaces, in order from left to right and top to bottom, so you're in the know before you go.

W	D	U	H	L	T	X
I	R	V	M	A	Y	T
J	E	P	B	O	C	D
K	V	Y	E	T	W	R
H	X	S	J	X	T	U
F	R	W	F	I	B	H
V	B	N	D	J	G	Y

To get the most from a trip to a different island,
you'll want to have this:

_ _ _ _ _ _ _ _ _ _   _ _ _ _ _ _   _ _ _ _ _ _ _ _

Trait Trails

Use the ladder maze to learn what kind of animal each character is and what their personality is like. Begin at the dot below each name and follow the trail downward. Every time you hit a horizontal trail (one that goes across), you must take it. Add your answers to the chart.

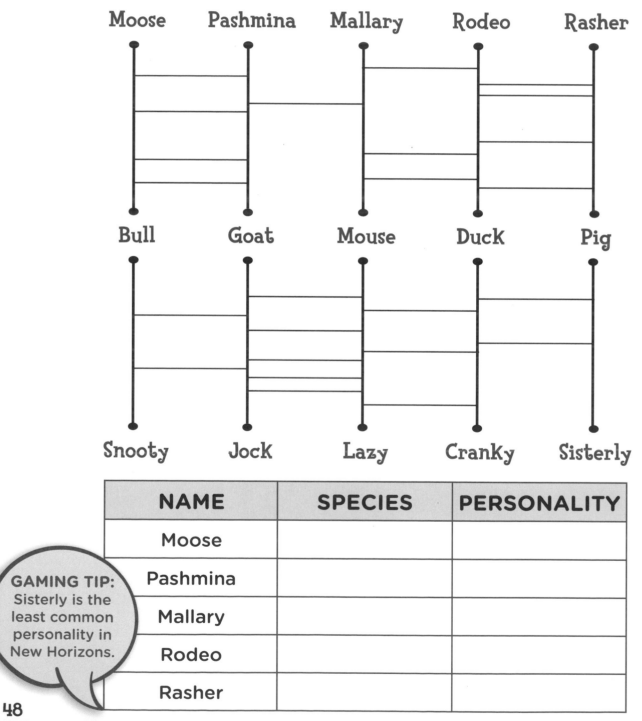

NAME	SPECIES	PERSONALITY
Moose		
Pashmina		
Mallary		
Rodeo		
Rasher		

GAMING TIP: Sisterly is the least common personality in New Horizons.

48

Net Results

Find the path that allows you to pick up all five tree branches you need to make a bug-catching net at the finish.

START

GAMING TIP: Craft your flimsy net into a regular net when you get an iron nugget.

Holiday Hoopla

Boxes connected by lines contain the same letter. Some letters are given, but others have to be guessed. Fill in all the boxes to reveal some New Horizons holidays and special events. Are these on your calendar?

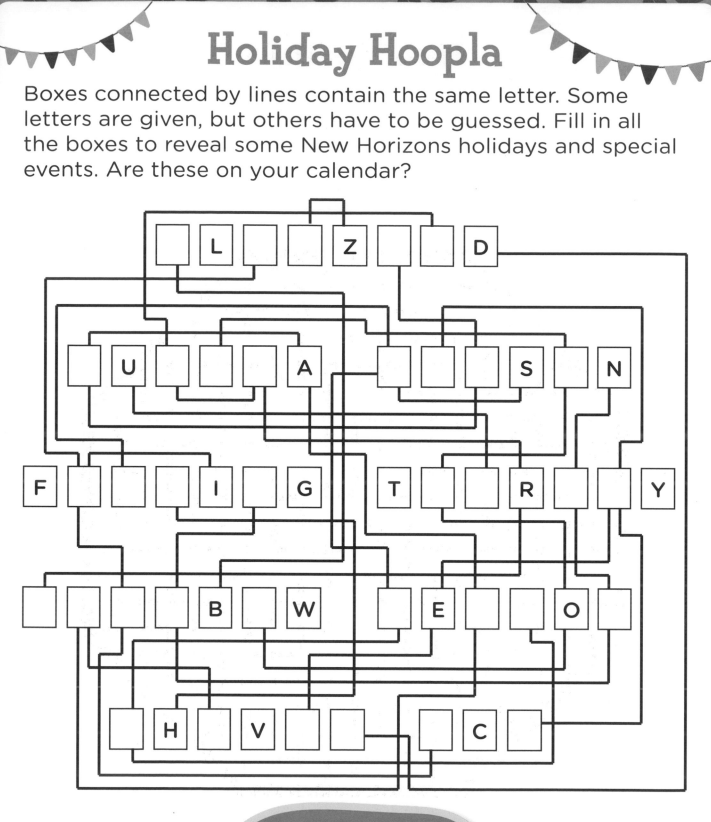

GAMING TIP:
Temporary villagers might visit during holidays and special events.

Encore

It's Saturday night and time for a jam session with K. K. Slider! The six song titles below are on the set list, but there's one more song he'll play. Place the titles in the crossword grid. Use the number of letters and intersecting letters to figure out where each word logically fits. The first one is done for you. Transfer the numbered letters to the spaces at the bottom of the page and discover the bonus song title.

7 Letters	8 Letters
HYPNO K. K.	FAREWELL
K. K. SYNTH	I LOVE YOU
MY PLACE	K. K. BAZAAR

GAMING TIP: K. K. Slider is a white dog (a Jack Russell Terrier!) who can play the guitar pretty well.

The bonus song is

$\overline{11}$ $\overline{12}$ $\overline{2}$ $\overline{8}$ $\overline{3}$ $\overline{5}$ $\overline{12}$ $\overline{9}$ $\overline{3}$ $\overline{1}$ $\overline{7}$ $\overline{10}$ $\overline{3}$ $\overline{4}$ $\overline{6}$

Puzzle Tourney

Write the letters of the correct pieces on the spaces to reveal a phrase C. J. the bear might use in a New Horizons fishing tourney. Heads up: pieces might be rotated or flipped, and not all pieces are used.

GAMING TIP:
Join C. J. for a fishing tournament the second Saturday of January, April, July, and October.

More Bells, Please

Start at the ↓. Write every third letter on the spaces until all have been used. If you place them correctly, you'll reveal a tip for getting more bells.

G _ _ _ _ _ _ _   _ _ _ _ _   -   _ _ _ _ _ _ _

_ _ _ _ _ _ _ _ _ _ _ _

New Horizons MVCs

Boxes connected by lines contain the same letter. Some letters are given, but others have to be guessed. Fill in all the boxes to reveal the five Most Valuable Critters in New Horizons.

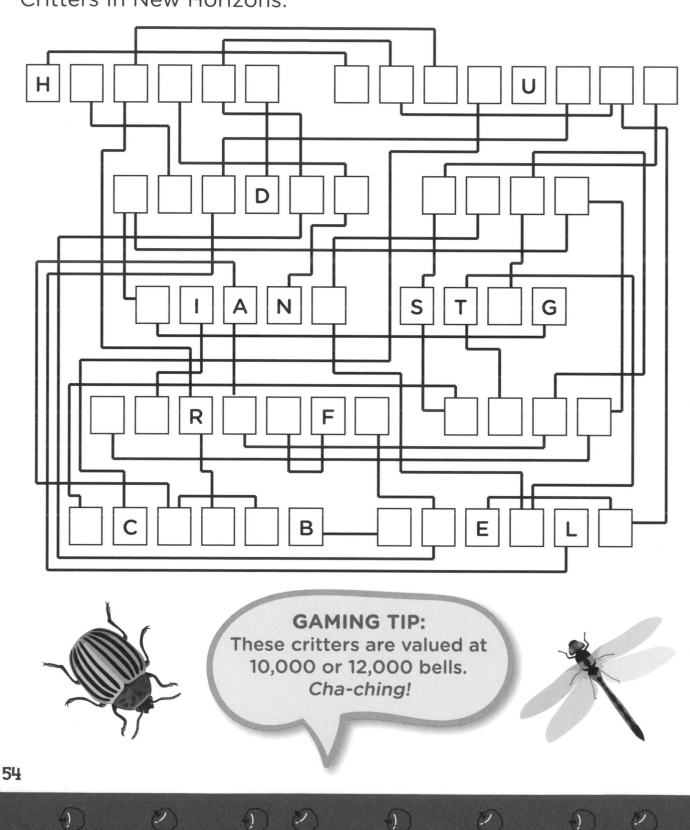

GAMING TIP:
These critters are valued at 10,000 or 12,000 bells. *Cha-ching!*

Permitted

One of these Animal Crossing New Horizons players has a permit to construct a cliff. Find your way through the maze to find out which one.

GAMING TIP: With the Island Designer app you can pave paths, build cliffs, and dig waterways.

ANSWER KEY

FIND YOUR DREAM BED (Page 4)

FAST TRACK GAMING (Page 5)

PRESS B TO RACE THROUGH TEXT

If you know Tom Nook's fish jokes by heart, and you're short on time, you can speed through them.

CRAFTY NEIGHBORS (Page 6)

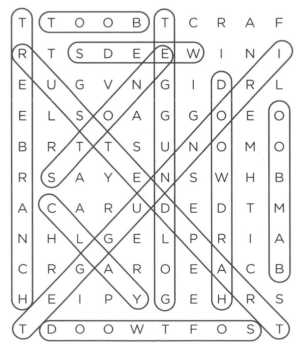

CRAFTY NEIGHBORS (continued)

CRAFTING VILLAGERS MAY SHARE THEIR RECIPES

So go talk to them!

THE GIFT OF GAB (Page 7)

Use this to chat with friends in-game: NOOK LINK

It's an app.

WHO'S WHO (Page 8)

ISABELLE - Resident Services Assistant

BLATHERS - Museum Curator

REDD - Art Seller

ORVILLE - Airline Clerk

TOM NOOK - Head of Resident Services

RECIPE FOR RECYCLING (Page 9)

1 empty can
1 boot
1 iron nugget

Recycled Can Thumb Piano

1 empty can
1 boot
1 old tire

Succulent Plant

1 empty can
2 boots
1 book

Trash Bags

1 empty can + 1 boot + 1 old tire = trash bags

FOSSIL FINDER (Page 10)

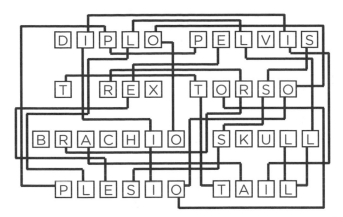

WAND-ERING (Page 14)

CRANKY CHARACTERS (Page 11)

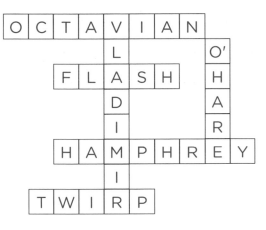

In New Horizons, cranky characters have LOW-PITCHED VOICES.

PIECE OF WISDOM (Page 12)

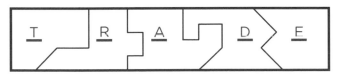

For items you want or need, go to a friend's island and TRADE.

ART APPRAISAL 1 (Page 13)

ONE TO GROWN ON (Page 15)

Planting a coconut grows a palm tree!

MONEY ROCK MYSTERY (Page 16)

The gray rock in the bottom row, center column is the money rock.

RESOURCE RADAR (Page 17)

Sparkle spots, Earth stars, and water spouts are GREAT PLACES TO DIG.

You'll find different resources to add to your inventory in all of these places.

CATCH THIS (Page 18)

CATCH ALL THESE CRITTERS WHILE THEY FLY

Some bugs are caught on the ground or on flowers, but these are all caught in flight.

THE POWER OF THREE (Page 19)

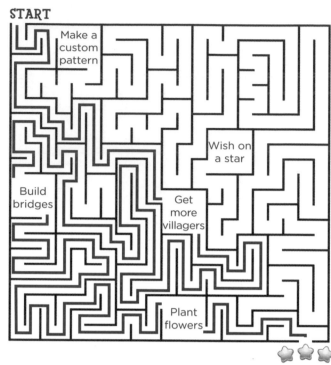

Some ways to get to a three-star rating include building bridges, planting flowers, and getting more villagers.

MESSAGE IN A . . . *MATH PROBLEM?* (Page 20)

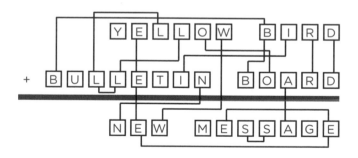

Get it? A yellow bird plus a bulletin board equals a new message. When there's a yellow bird on the bulletin board outside Resident Services, it means there is an announcement you haven't seen.

Bonus tip: At night there's a white owl instead of a yellow bird.

TOOLING AROUND (Page 21)

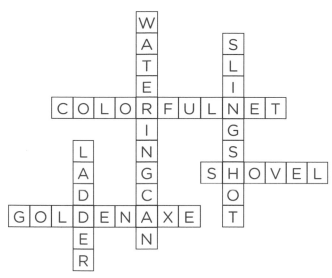

This tool will keep you organized and ready to act in a jiffy: TOOL RING

After you pay off your bill for getting to the island, you can purchase the tool ring from the Nook Stop for just 800 Nook Miles.

CHA-CHING (Page 22)

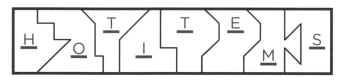

HOT ITEMS

Check the bulletin board outside Nook's Cranny to see what the Hot Item is. It changes daily. You can sell this item to Timmy for twice its usual price.

MOOD MASTER (Page 23)

Sadness   Shocked

Delight   Greetings

Anger   Joy

DODO DESTSINATIONS (Page 24)

JILLIBEAN: Rare flower Island
BELL FARMER: Tarantula Island
SPARKLE FERRET: Bamboo Island

MAKE IT YOURS (Page 25)

MAKE CUSTOM PATTERNS FROM YOUR PHOTOS

Turn your favorite photo into a mural using the Nintendo Switch Online app for Android or iOS.

YEAR-ROUND RESIDENTS (Page 26)

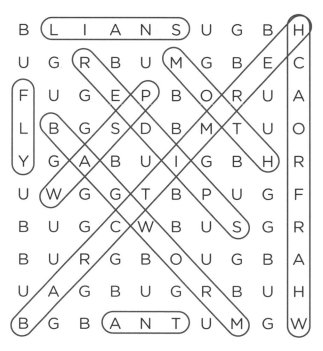

The mystery word is BUG.

GET RICH QUICK! (Page 27)

If you can do this in New Horizons, you'll get rich quick!

TURNIP GOAL: BUY LOW, SELL HIGH

If you can buy turnips from Daisy Mae at a low price and sell them at Nook's Cranny for a higher price, you could make big bells. Of course, you can't control the buying and selling prices, so . . . that could be a problem!

ART APPRAISAL 2 (Page 28)

GREEN THUMB ENTERPRISE
(Page 29)

To grow a money tree and triple your bells, find the glowing spot, dig up 1,000 bells, and plant 10,000 bells.

CONNECT THE DOTS (Page 30)

RAY

THE GREATEST ROCK HITS
(Page 31)

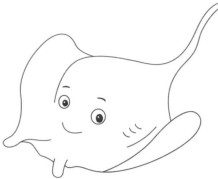

Do this to ensure you can hit a rock 8 times quickly: DIG TWO HOLES

Digging holes behind you to the left and behind you to the right (catty-corner to where you stand) will prevent you from being knocked too far backward when you hit the rock, allowing you to reach the rock each time you swing without having to step closer.

YOU'RE INVITED! (Page 32)

DODO CODE

This is a code you can give or receive to play Animal Crossing New Horizons online with a friend or even a group.

FISHING SKILLS CHALLENGE
(Page 33)

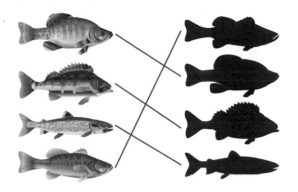

STARRY NIGHT (Page 34)

TEMPORARY TREATS (Page 35)

GRAB ONE-OF-A-KIND ITEMS AT SPECIAL EVENTS

Holidays and special events offer unique treats that aren't available at any other time. Don't miss them!

TENT DILEMMA (Page 36)

Your friend wants tent #8.

MAXED MUSEUM (Page 37)

If you want a complete museum collection, you'll have to do this:
PLAY YEAR-ROUND

Some museum specimens are only available seasonally, so to get them all, you'll need to collect year-round.

SAY WHAT? (Page 38)

These "words" are all CATCHPHRASES.

All villagers have them. Do you know the catchphrases of the villagers on your island? What would your catchphrase be?

TULIP TIME (Page 39)

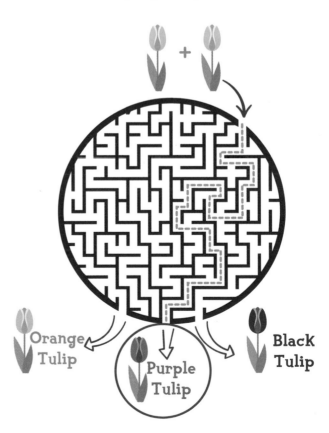

WHAT'S SHAKIN'? (Page 40)

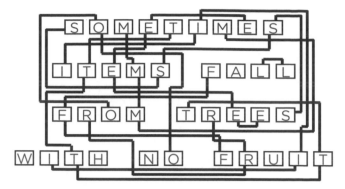

So shake trees whether they have fruit or not. Of course, watch out for wasps, too.

NOT FOR SALE (Page 41)

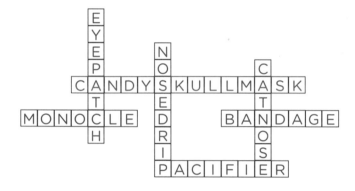

If you give away your BIRTHDAY CUPCAKES, you might get BIRTHDAY SHADES.

When you give your cupcakes to villagers, they'll give you birthday presents.

SELF IMPROVEMENT (Page 42)

A MIRROR

Once you have a mirror, you can change your hair style, eyes, nose, and mouth.

ART APPRAISAL 3 (Page 43)

CONNECT THE DOTS (Page 44)

AIRPLANE

HEADS UP: INCOMING (Page 45)

LISTEN FOR A WHISTLING BREEZE

That's what floating balloons sound like. If your sound is on, you can hear balloon presents coming.

WHAT'S "NORMAL"? (Page 46)

A common interest shared by "normal" characters is THEY ALL LIKE TO READ.

KNOW BEFORE YOU GO (Page 47)

To get the most from a trip to a different island, you'll want to have this: ULTIMATE POCKET STUFFING

So you can bring home more *stuff*, see? It's available at the Nook Stop for 8,000 miles. Did we get you with that T? It appears four times, so it doesn't get crossed off. Tricky, tricky!

TRAIT TRAILS (Page 48)

Name	Species	Personality
Moose	Mouse	Jock
Pashmina	Goat	Sisterly
Mallary	Duck	Snooty
Rodeo	Bull	Lazy
Rasher	Pig	Cranky

NET RESULTS (Page 49)

START

HOLIDAY HOOPLA (Page 50)

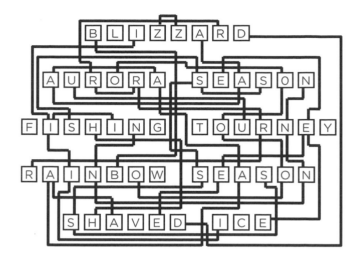

ENCORE (Page 51)

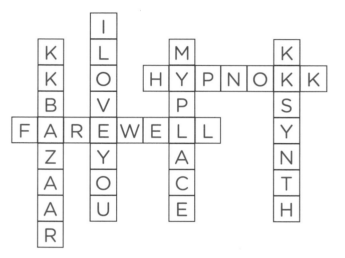

The encore K. K. Slider will play—if you came up with the right title—is WELCOME HORIZONS.

PUZZLE TOURNEY (Page 52)

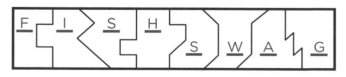

FISH SWAG

Fish swag are special items offered by C. J. during fishing tournaments to participants who earn 10 or more points.

MORE BELLS, PLEASE (Page 53)

GROW NON-NATIVE FRUITS TO SELL

Fruits that were growing on your island when you arrived (native fruits) sell for 100 bells. Fruits that are not native to your island sell for 500 bells.

NEW HORIZONS MVCS (Page 54)

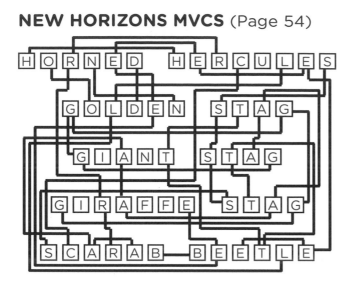

PERMITTED (Page 55)